101 Great Drinking Games

Andrew Stuttard

Published by Brewery Products, PO Box 168, Leatherhead, Surrey KT22 8YJ

First Published 1992

© Brewery Products, 1992

ISBN 0 9520650 0 2

Cartoons by Hamish Buchanan

Designed and typeset by Language & Publishing Solutions

Note:- The author recommends that none of the games in this book are to be played using alcohol because if drank to excess this can cause loss of balance, blurred speech, double vision, memory loss etc etc.

Contents

Introduction

How many times have you been sitting in a bar or at a dinner party and wished the 'action' would liven up? Well this book gives you the chance to really liven events up wherever you may happen to be. It is an ideal companion to any night out but you must remember that things tend to get a little out of hand the longer the Book is open!!?!

The Book is about having a cracking night out with games to suit all kinds of occasions and all kinds of people, (as long as they are prepared for raucous behaviour)!!?!

The research needed for such a book has taken a number of years and led me into many a dingy bar in the 'quest' for the ultimate drinking game. Each game has been tried and tested several times by a whole host of friends and we have certainly had a lot of fun playing them. I would like to thank all those friends who have

Ice Breakers!!!

helped contribute towards the book and especially Dave Roberts and George Blakeway. A special thanks must go to Hamish Buchanan for the brilliant cartoons in the book, which were produced within a very limited timescale.

Throughout the book I have generally referred to the participants as 'he' because using both 'he' and 'she' would prove both cumbersome and very awkward. I hope that this does not upset anyone or take anything away from your enjoyment of the book. I hope you all have a fantastic time playing the varied games and below I have set out a few of the words and expressions used throughout the book, so that you can familiarize yourselves straight away.

The Chairman:- This is the person in charge of running the game.

The Chief Sneak:- The second in command of the game and it is his job to report to the Chairman any mistakes or bad behaviour made during play.

The Judge:- A much respected 'pillar' of the drinking community. He will be called in if there is a particularly unsavoury incident which needs his 'special' judgement.

International Rules:- These are the rules which all participants must adhere to during play and they are; left handed drinking only; the Chairman can not be directly spoken to and he must be approached through the Chief Sneak using a predetermined sign. If the Chief Sneak makes a mistake then this is the only time the Chairman may be contacted directly and once again a predetermined sign must be used. No swearing or riotous behaviour allowed during play. Generally no pointing allowed except with your elbow.

Fines:- These are usually fingers of a drink, for example, line your fingers up against the liquid in your glass and drink to the bottom of one, two or three fingers etc etc.

Boy:- 'Boy' is another way of being fined and it means that you have to act as a waiter for your friends, plus have to wear your clothes inside out for the whole evening!!?!

Note:- The author recommends that none of the games in this book are to be played using alcohol because if drank to excess this can cause loss of balance, blurred speech, double vision, memory loss etc etc.

I
Evening Openers

Most people when they first go out in the evening like to get off to a cracking pace. This chapter provides a number of games which are short and come straight to the point. They provide many laughs and if they are played for prolonged periods then they can be extremely devastating!!?! You have been warned!!?!

1 · Next

Both a simple and quick game which requires two or more people and is an excellent evening opener.

The first player stands up and consumes his glass (which must be full) in one go. When finished he must select another player, point to him and shout 'next.' This player must then drink his glass and the game continues until all players have finished their drinks.

It is very unusual to play this game more than two or three times in one evening!!?!

2 · The Funnel

You need a large funnel with about a metre long tube attached to the end of it. One person holds the funnel up in the air, while the person about to drink has the tube ready in his mouth. Then a drink is placed in the top and down she goes with no time to think.

Often during the playing of this game you can be a bit cheeky by having someone continuously pouring liquid in the top which the person drinking generally does not spot until he feels his bladder about to give way!!?!

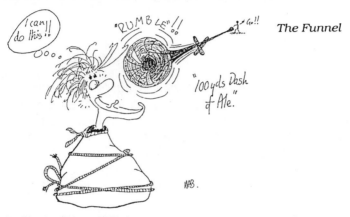

The Funnel

3 · Fizz Buzz Whizz

Two or more players are required.

A mathematical game which will certainly require a degree of intelligence and therefore it is best to play it before the more raucous behaviour starts!!?!

Stand or sit in a circle. Player one starts with the words 'to my left (or right) 1.' The player to his left (or right) responds immediately with 2 and so on around the circle. Sounds simple? Any number which contains a 3, for example 3, 13, 23, 30, 31 etc, or any number which is a multiple of 3 for example 9, 12, 15 etc, the player must say 'Fizz'. For fives or multiples of 5 the player must say 'Buzz' and for sevens or multiples of 7, 'Whizz'. A number such as 15 which is both a multiple of 3 and 5 plus contains a 5 the player must say 'Fizz Buzz Buzz' or in the case of 21 'Fizz Wizz'. 35 would be Fizz, (contains a 3) Buzz, (contains a five) Buzz, (multiple of 5) and Whizz (multiple of 7). So 35 is Fizz Buzz Buzz Whizz!!?!

An example sequence:- 1, 2 Fizz, 4, Buzz, Fizz, Whizz, 8, Fizz, Buzz, 11, Fizz, Fizz, Whizz, Fizz Buzz Buzz, 16 etc ...

Any failure to respond immediately with the correct number or word results in that player drinking a fine of his drink. Alternatively that player can take a fine and drop out of the circle until two players battle it out for the win.

This does become easier the more you play the game. When extremely proficient, use any 'Whizz' to change the direction of the game!!?!

4 · Heads or Tails

This is both a simple and effective game and best played with two or more people.

To play one person flicks a coin and the next person without looking has to say if he thinks it is heads or tails. If he predicts wrongly then he drinks a finger but if he is correct then the person flicking the coin quaffs. The person flicking the coin will continue until he has flicked against all the participants.

This game is best played with small fines because it is a very quick and demanding game which will put you in great voice for the more vociferous games to come later on!!?!

5 · Fingers and Toes

This is a game for two people only. You sit opposite each other with your heels together and your feet pointing out at an angle touching one another.

Rest a glass on the chair between your thighs, then get a matchbox and using your forefingers of both hands as pivots, rest the matchbox between the thumbs, then you must try and flick the matchbox into your opponents drink. Each time you succeed, your opponent will have to down two fingers unless he can get the matchbox into your glass with his next try which results in four fingers to you.The fingers keep on accumulating until someone misses.

This can be a very punishing and nerve tingling game!!?!

6 · High Stakes

You need a group of you for this game and a pack of cards. One card is dealt to each player and the player must not look at it, but immediately put it on his forehead facing the other participants.

Then each person bets a certain number of fingers with the person who has got the highest card winning, while the rest have to drink however many fingers the winner gambled, plus their own stake. (Aces are low in this game). For example, if there are four people playing and the cards facing you are a '4,' a '5,' and a '3' then you would probably bet fairly high, maybe four fingers because you have a very good chance of winning. If your card is higher, then everyone drinks the four fingers you bet plus their own individual bets as well. A lot of drink may well be consumed if you are too rash with your betting!!?!

7 · Scrambled Eggs

A game involving two people and a box of free range eggs.

The two participants each have one egg and stand three paces apart. They then, at the same time throw the eggs underarm to each other, hopefully catching them!!?! If they succeed then they take a step back and do exactly the same thing.

Each completed egg throw then results in one step back and two fingers of your chosen drink.

This is a very messy but fun game, especially as time wears on!!?!

8 · Hic Hac Hoc

A very quick game for two or more people and a game to use to set the evening alight!!?!

To play you need to use your hands to make one of three objects; either a stone (clenched fist); a piece of paper (flat palm), or a pair of scissors (index and middle finger pointing out). With these symbols a stone will blunt scissors, scissors cut paper and paper wraps stone. All you do is whoever is playing puts their fists out in the middle, and then you say 'hic hac hoc' and on the 'hoc' you produce one of the above symbols.

For example, if there are three people playing and two of them produce scissors while the other goes paper, then the two people win and the loser has to drink, therefore scissors cuts paper. Also if one player produces stone and the other two go scissors, then the first person wins and the other two would play again to see who loses, therefore stone blunts scissors.

It is also a great game to decide many problems like for example who is going to pay for the curry or who is going to answer the phone etc!!?!

If a number of people are playing (six or more), then it is best to have a semi-final and then a final.

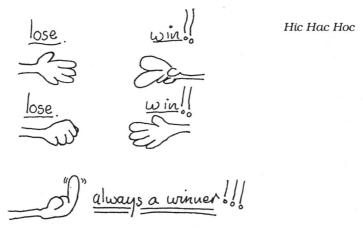

Hic Hac Hoc

9 · 4 Jacks

An old favourite of every stag night and once featured in an edition of East-Enders, this simple game is an excellent kick-start to every evening. You require two or more players and a pack of cards to be able to start.

One player shuffles the cards and proceeds to deal each player one card face up. This continues until a jack is turned up. The player who has received this first jack must choose a long drink. The player receiving the second jack must choose a chaser to add to that drink. The third jack means that unfortunate player must pay for the drink, and the final jack spells disaster for that player as he must then consume the beverage!!?!

Beware:- If it is your stag night, watch the dealer carefully as it has been known that all the jacks can appear at your seat - uncanny!!?!

10 · Luck of the Draw

All you do for this game is have a stack of coins, then each person must predict if the next coin is going to be 'heads' or 'tails' and every time he is wrong he has to drink two fingers. The coins will keep on turning until he has predicted the next coin correctly. A short and sweet game which, if your luck is out, can get your evening off to a disastrous start depending on your views!!?!

11 · Russian Roulette

You need six cans of drink and six participants. Shake up one of the cans and place them all in a bag so they are mixed up. One by one take a can out of the bag and open it in front of your face so it is pointing directly at you, and about six inches away. Obviously one of the six will have the shaken can, and it will explode in his face!!?!

Whoever this happens to, suffers the indignity of drink all over his face, plus have to down the remainder in his can!!?!

Russian Roulette

12 · Draw Hic Hac Hoc

This is basically a variation on the normal 'Hic Hac Hoc' (explained earlier). You each take it in turn to draw your hand out from behind your back first and produce either paper, scissors or stone. Then the other players must try and beat what you have produced.

For example, if stone is drawn, then the winner will be the first to draw paper. If scissors or stone are drawn then that would automatically mean a drinking fine.

This is a quick fire game and because of this it tends to produce a lot of errors on the draw. Often the participants try and predict the call before it has been made and thus invariably come unstuck!!?!

13 · Higher or Lower

This is played along the same lines as 'Heads or Tails,' except that a pack of cards is used. You turn one card over and then have to predict if the next card will be higher or lower. If you are right in your prediction then the game carries onto the next person. If you are wrong then you must take a two finger fine and continue until you succeed. If the value of the card turned over is the same as your card, then you automatically lose. Finally Aces are always counted as high.

14 · Word Association

A simple quickfire game but as the evening wears on it inevitably becomes a lot harder!!?! What you do is someone picks an object and the next person has to say a word connected to this object.

For example the word might be 'tree' and the next person might say 'wood' and then the next person 'worm' etc etc.
  Any hesitations, obscure connections and stupidity are all punishable by large quantities of drink!!?!

15 · Four Heads

The name gives a pretty clear indication of the game. One coin is required and a circle of people. One player will toss the coin, catch it and flick it onto the back of the other hand so that it is still covered. (This is not so important early on, but will become clear later.) They then have a look at it. If it is heads they will call one head, or if it is tails they call no heads. The coin is then passed on, and any heads gained added on. When there are three heads, the tension mounts because if the next call is a heads, for example four heads, the last person to put their hand to their forehead must drink four fingers!!?!

If this is a bit tame for you, you can add that every time the coin is tossed it must make contact with the roof/ceiling and be caught in the left hand otherwise a fine will be called for!!?!

16 · The Shot Gun

All you do here is a simple 'hic hac hoc,' (explained earlier), to see who goes first. The person who loses gets a can, makes a small hole in the bottom of it which he covers with his finger, then opens the top of the can making sure his mouth is covering the hole in the bottom. You will soon see and feel the result!!?!

If any spillage results then I am afraid another can must be 'shot gunned' until it is consumed perfectly!!?!

The Shot Gun

17 · Over and Out

This game provides a few laughs because often people reckon they are a little bit tougher than they actually are. This game sorts out 'the men from the boys!!?!'

What you need is two bar-stools and a bottle. You have to rest your ankles on one bar-stool and your head on the other, so you are fully stretched out. Then you have to see how many times you can pass a bottle over and under your body. This is a hard and tiring exercise to attempt and the winner, the person who does it the most times, fully deserves the drinks that the losers must buy him!!?!

18 · Whose Line Is It

This is a game of improvisation which can be played almost anywhere and during any circumstances.

What you do is pick up an object and each person has to think up a use for that object.

For example you could be at a party and you might stumble across a spoon. We all know that a spoon could be used as a beautiful 'silver' earring, a handy little ear cleaner, a cheeky little cap. Also someone might give you a pencil, how could you improvise? Maybe a suave little 'pencil' thin moustache or a handy conductors baton etc!!?!

Anyone who does not show enough imagination has to drink and anyone too sensible with their ideas should take a severe fine!!?!

19 · Chase the Ace

A tactical game, easily played at any stage of the evening. The object of the game is to avoid having the lowest card.

One player shuffles the cards and deals one card, face down, to each player. The player to the dealers left then looks at his card, without showing it to anyone else. If he is sufficiently happy with his card he can elect to keep it (usually if it is over 8 or 9), if he is concerned that it is low then he can swop his card for the one held by the player to his left. If he elects to swop then he must keep the card he gains from his adjacent player. The next player then has the same options, for example, either to keep his card or swop with the player to his left. This continues until everyone has had the opportunity to swop, the dealer having no opportunity. The cards are then turned over and the player holding the lowest card must perform the agreed forfeit, for example buying a round, drinking two fingers etc. Each player takes a turn to deal so that each person has the opportunity to start.

Aces are low hence the name of the game and they tend to be passed right round the table, ending up at the dealer!!?! However, there is one extra rule which can be a life-saver. If a player holds a king, then he can refuse to swop as the king is unbeatable. This means that a player cannot pass on a low card as he is 'blocked' by a player holding a king and he is therefore forced to keep the card he holds.

20 · The Bollocks Game

Another strange but brilliant game and best played with about half a dozen people in a crowded place. All you do is one person starts by saying 'Bollocks' quite quietly and each person in turn must say 'Bollocks' louder than the person before. Anyone deemed not to have said it louder will be punished by drink.

This game tends to annoy certain sections of a bar/pub and so it is best not to perform 'it' in some cosy little wine bar in the heart of the city unless you wish to leave rather quickly!!?!

The Bollocks Game

II
Set Up Games

I did not think any drinking games book would
have been complete without including a chapter
on setting people up. Wherever you go there will
always be somebody gullible enough to be set
up, but the great thing about this section is that
all the games are extremely well disguised. As
long as everyone plays along then the 'victim' will
not 'cotton on' until it is too late!!?!

All these 'Set up Games' are meant to be
light-hearted and the 'victim' will only suffer a
tiny bit of humiliation!!?!

21 · Bomber Command

This is a superb set up game involving a large number of
people who know the trick and one innocent party who is a
little bit naive!!?!

The idea is to pretend you are a 'Lancaster' bomber on a
mission to bomb the 'Hun.' Therefore you need four people
to act as propellers on the plane who sit down on chairs all in
a line. You then need a forward gunner and a rear gunner
plus a pilot, who all spread themselves along the plane. Then
finally you need a 'bomb,' who is the victim, and he should

be sat right in the middle of the plane, so he is sitting between all the participants.

Once everybody is in place the pilot starts the propellers one by one, and thus the people swing their arms around in propeller-like motions. The plane then takes off and everyone involved in the plane leans back in their chairs. Then the plane banks right, so everyone leans right, and then it banks left and so everyone leans left. The pilot then spots enemy aircraft; 'Bandits at 2 o'clock Squiffy' he shouts, and at that point the gunners fire their imaginative guns and make gun like noises. Suddenly the plane gets hit and the pilot shouts;

'fire in the bomb bay,'

and at this point the gunners, the pilot and all those acting as propellers throw their drinks over the bomb in the bomb bay to put the fire out, thus soaking the unfortunate individual. This is a classic game for a packed out bar/club and guaranteed to create havoc!!?!

22 · The 3 Man Lift

A superb game to play on an unsuspecting person. It is best played in a busy bar.

You need three people who know the trick and one victim. One of the three has to pretend he is really strong and boast to everyone that he is capable of lifting up three people!!?! He then invites the victim to lie flat on his back in front of him and the other two 'cronies' to lie on either side, making sure they all interlock arms. Then the so-called 'strongman' asks for the victims belt so he can make sure the attempted lift is totally secure.

With the victim helpless, the 'strongman' then grabs a drink and pours it down the victim's trousers and that is the '3 Man Lift.' Total humiliation!!?!

PS. The bigger the build up, the better it works. For example, if you go out for an evening with some friends and you wish to play the trick on one of them, then it is best to conspire against one person. This is done by really building up the 'mystique' of the '3 Man Lift' by suggesting that tonight could be the night to attempt 'it' because you are feeling really strong. Someone is bound to fall for this and then, 'voila,' the trap has been laid!!?!

23 · The Parachute Jump
This is a game to set up an unsuspecting victim.

You need two strong men and two trays. The victim, who is the parachutist, stands blind-folded on a sturdy tray. He is told that he will be raised high on the tray, and when he feels his head touch the ceiling he must jump.

The two strong men pick up the tray and raise it waist high and then they drop slowly to a crouching position. The parachutist, at this stage believes he is ascending as he feels them drop beneath him, but really he is only a couple of inches from the ground.

By now he should be having reservations and to scare him a fraction more, it is best to tilt the tray a little or wobble it!!?!

Once the tray bearers are at their crouching position, another person then brings a second tray down to rest on the parachutist's head. The parachutist believes he has reached the ceiling so he prepares to leap and take the full force of the drop. Then, as he jumps, it is to much public amusement when he has only jumped two inches or so!!?!

The Parachute Jump

24 · Blow Football

A great game to set two people up.

You need a tray, two straws, a peanut and a lot of water.
   You get two volunteers who have never seen the game/trick before and a referee. The two volunteers sit opposite each other at a table, and between them is a tray filled with water and a peanut floating in the middle. They reckon that it is just a simple game of blow football and so they are all set with their straws poised for action. The referee tells them that on the count of three they must start blowing. Therefore the two volunteers are ready for action and on the count of three, the referee brings his hand down on the tray and completely soaks the two volunteers!!?!

25 · Thumper

This game can involve severe pain for the person who has to endure it.

What you do is that you tell the victim that a coin is to be 'forced' to stick on his forehead, with the object being to see how many hits on the back of the head it takes to dislodge

Thumper

the coin. You give a demonstration and after a few gentle hits the coin comes off your forehead.

The victim will be thinking how easy that all looks, and thus you offer to put the coin on his forehead, pushing it on hard. But really you do not put the coin there at all, but to the victim it feels like it is there and he will 'bang' away for some time until you show him the coin and then he realises!!?!

26 · Kissing the Blarney Stone

'Blarney' is a castle and town in County Cork, Ireland, and within the castle is what is known as the 'Blarney' stone. This stone is reputed to confer eloquence on those who kiss it. With this in mind this set up game should take place in a crowded bar or party.

To start the game you have to convince the 'victim' about the magical powers of the stone and the honour it will bring to visit it. Once this has been achieved you can begin.

The victim is asked to sit on a stool with a blindfold on. First of all he has to fly to Southern Ireland, so the stool is picked up by four people dragged along the ground, (simulating take off), then lifted up and taken around the room finally landing in Southern Ireland with a bump. Throughout all this the victim will be hanging on for dear life .

Once he has landed safely he must then embark upon a horse and cart ride to the castle. So once again the stool is shook up, down and around before arriving at the castle. Then he is helped off the stool, still with his blindfold on, and there in front of him is the 'Blarney' stone. At this point you need someone (preferably with a hairy arm), to bend one of their arms, the victim is then asked to kiss the flesh of the arm just above the elbow. The blindfold is then removed and just at that point you need a man to be walking away doing his trousers up. Thus the victim believes he has just kissed the man's ... and invariably runs out of the pub!!?!

27 · Broom Game

Equipment needed:- One broom, two chairs/tables, and a length of rope, cloth or a soft belt, tied into a small loop. (The length of the loop to be approximately two feet.)

An excellent pub trick to be played on an unsuspecting individual.

The best way to do this is for an 'experienced' player to go first. The 'idea' of the game is to see how many twists the player can put in the length of rope.

Get the player to squat down and place a broom handle behind his knees and in front of his elbows. Then place the loop of rope over his wrists asking him to clench his fists. Ask the player to see how many times he can twist the rope by revolving one of his wrists. The process will continually shorten the length of rope until no more twists are possible and the wrists are actually almost tied together. As the player twists the rope, get the audience to 'count' and so encourage him to tighten the rope. If the experienced person has gone first, ask a 'novice' to try and beat it. When the novice declares he has (having tightened the loop) get two experienced players to grab one end of the broom each, and support each end on a table or chair, so leaving the player dangling from the broom, and due to his weight on the loop he will not be able to move. Leave the player there for sufficient time for everyone to have a good laugh (suggest at least twenty minutes)!!?!

28 · The Hands of Fate

These determine how many fingers a person should drink.

If someone has been fined or found guilty of doing a stupid caper like getting engaged or scoring a hatrick of tries/goals, then the 'Hands of Fate' can come into operation. The 'Hands of Fate' are a panel of three people who each hold up their hands in a waving motion and when they stop, how ever many fingers they are holding up is the fine that person must drink!!?!

A little rhyme tends to accompany the 'Hands of Fate' and it goes:- 'The Hands of Fate, here they go where they stop, nobody knows!!?!' At the end of this rhyme, the victims fate will be known!!?!

29 · The Court Case

The Court Case is the main way of trying a foolish or stupid individual who has committed an offence which is deemed to have gone beyond the bounds of human tolerance. For example, a man might be charged for being a continual pest/deliberate offender during a drinking game, or a man might be charged for deliberately avoiding buying a round of drinks. (Excuses for this latter offence range from, 'I have to phone my mum up,' to, 'oh I have no money,' - pathetic and you all know such an individual!!?!)

Once someone is hauled in front of the court, the case is then presided over by a Judge who tends to be a respected member of the drinking community. As well as the Judge there should be a prosecutor and occasionally a defence lawyer. (Who more than likely will plead guilty for his client anyway!!?!).

Once all the evidence has been heard, then the jury, normally all those watching the proceedings, will deliver their verdict. This is done by either a thumbs up for a verdict of not guilty (unlikely!!?!), or a thumbs down for a guilty verdict (very likely!!?!). Sentence will then be passed by the unbiased Judge. Judges these days tend to be 'harsh but fair,' but with particularly unsavoury individuals they tend to err on the harsh side.

If a judge is undecided on the fine to be dished out then the 'Hands of Fate' can be brought in for the ultimate drinking decision!!?!

30 · The Spoon Game

Two players are required, one who is in on the trick and the other who is the victim. They must kneel or sit opposite each other and be fairly close with a tablespoon sticking out of their mouths, held in by their teeth.

You then explain that in turn each one must bend over forward and allow the other to hit him on the back of the head with the spoon, but only by holding it in their mouths. This should continue and the loser is the first to drop out. This would actually carry on for some time as it does not really hurt, but the trick is you have someone with a large ladle standing behind the victim. When the victim's head is down and as the other player brings his spoon down the person with the ladle gives the victim a good crack on the head. He obviously thinks it is the other player and tries to get his own back by continuing the game, which unfortunately only leads to his further suffering. Great fun for everyone around but not so good for the victim. Unlucky!!?!

31 · Cheeky Cheeky

This is a great set up game involving a large crowd and one
unlucky victim!!?!

Everyone stands in a large circle with the chairman standing
in the middle giving out the orders. To start with he might say,
'touch the cheek of the person on your left with your right
hand.' In turn everyone does this and says 'cheeky cheeky'
as they are doing it. The chairman might then say 'touch the
nose of the person on your left with your right hand.' Once
again everyone does this in turn and everyone says 'nosey
nosey' as they are doing it. This carries on for a number of
facial features with the trick being that the person next to the
victim dabs his hand in ash in a ashtray everytime he does a
new command. Thus the victims face will gradually turn
grey!!?! The victim will not realise why everyone is laughing,
and to disguise it further the rest of the group must be called
into the middle of the circle to drink if they do not put
enough feeling into enacting the commands.

Once the victims face has been covered he must then be
informed and given a mirror!!?!

Cheeky Cheeky

III
Television Drinking Games

As we all know watching some excellent sport on the television, or watching one of the well established soaps is a great way to spend an afternoon or evening, but it can be made more enjoyable by playing drinking games during the proceedings.

In this small section I have included a number of games to play whilst watching the four main groups of sport shown on television, plus I have included a game to play whilst watching soaps.

---

32 · Drinking Whilst Watching Rugby/Football
In order to play this particular game you write down on individual bits of paper the numbers 1-30 or 1-22 depending on the sport, and these go into a hat to be picked out by the participants of the game.

Then it is simply each time any of your players are mentioned by the commentator you drink a finger, and if any of your players either score a try or a goal, three fingers must be consumed.

A harsh and exacting drinking game which tends to have dire consequences!!?!

33 · Drinking Whilst Watching Tennis

Another simple, but clinical game which definitely tests your tennis judgement!!?! It is an ideal game to wile away those hot barmy days during the Wimbledon fortnight!!?!

All you do is predict who is going to win the next point. If you are right then you do not have to drink but if you are wrong then a finger must be consumed. I would not recommend playing this game for too many sets for obvious reasons!!?!

34 · Drinking Whilst Watching Golf

As one of the fastest growing sports in Great Britain I thought it would be advisable to include this game. It enables all those armchair buffs who have never staggered further than the members clubhouse to participate in a drinking game. All you have to do is follow one golfer for one hole at a time and predict how many strokes he will take. If you are right then you do not drink, but if you guess incorrectly, then you must drink the difference.

For example, if you thought 'Seve' would get a par and he actually bagged a birdie then a finger must be consumed. Or if 'Woosie' took a bogey six and you predicted he would get a birdie four, then you would have to drink two fingers.

35 · Drinking Whilst Watching Cricket

This particular game should be played during five overs worth of play with definite rests between overs. Once again you have to predict what the next ball will bring, for example, 1 run, 2, 3, 4, 5, 6 runs; a wide; no ball; no runs; overthrow; leg byes or a wicket.

If you are correct in your prediction then it is minus fingers against your name, but if you predict wrongly then it is the difference between the score you predicted and the actual score. For example if you predict '1' run and it is a '4,' then it is three fingers, and if you predict a wide and it is '1' run then it is one finger to you. If you predict a '6' and this is correct then it is minus six fingers to you. Finally every time a wicket falls, it is automatically four fingers unless you predict this, then it is minus four fingers. All fines should be drunk at the end of a five over stretch.

It is probably not wise to play this game all day because
dire consequences could result!!?!

36 · Drinking Whilst Watching Soaps

Soaps probably originated in England, so I thought it only fair
to incorporate a rather fun drinking game I have often
played whilst watching numerous episodes of 'the Street'
and other such established soaps. It is probably not advisable
to play it during an episode of the BBC's latest offering
because let's face it, who wants to sit through an episode of
Eldorado!!?!

Anyway the game is once again a simple one in that every
time 'Bet' or one of the bar staff pulls a pint in 'the Street' you
must drink, and equally every time a pint is pulled in the
Queen Vic, Eastenders a drink must be consumed.

Also if you are watching one of those crass American
soaps, then every time JR pours a drink, or Ray Krebbs slurps
down one of his root beers then you must drink.

This is a fun game which must be strictly adhered to, but
Eldorado for me, is definitely off limits.

IV
Mass Participation Games

When large groups get together it is important that there are a surplus of games which will 'bond' the group together. This section certainly provides many great games which enable everyone to get involved. It is essential in this section for strong leadership and so for all you budding Chairmen now is your chance to take control!!?!

---

37 · Red Indians

This is a game for a large group of you and is best played at high speed.

Each player must think up a stupid/silly sign which he is to be recognised as during the game, and everyone must be told each others signs. For example your sign might be two fingers up your nose or two hands on your head etc etc. Once these have been established the game can commence.

You all sit around a table and drum your two index fingers up and down very quickly on the table, and then the chairman starts by doing his own signal and then randomly someone else's. The person he does then must do his own sign and then another persons. It goes around like this until a mistake is made, (which does not tend to be too long!!?!), with mistakes being punishable by drink. One rule is that you cannot use the sign of the person who has just nominated you.

Finally, the chairman can at any time shout, 'roll call,' and this means that everyone in turn must demonstrate their own sign to refresh everyone's memories.

38 · The Truth Game

This game is best played amongst a close group of friends because it can reveal some rather intimate secrets!!?!

One person starts the game by saying;

'I have never done something or been somewhere.'

For example 'I have never read the Sunday Sport.' All those who have read this 'quality' paper must drink a finger. All those who deny such an act, but someone remembers seeing them, must drink at least two fingers.

Also, and this is vitally important, if someone boasts of doing something and is actually lying then he must suffer a severe fine of four fingers. Lying in any form during a drinking game, is considered a rather heinous offence and you must pay a heavy fine for such transgressions!!?!

The Truth Game

39 · Wibbly/Wobbly

This is a great game for a large group of people.

You need two broom handles and each person must have a full drink. You line up in two teams and when the order is given the first team member of the two teams, downs his drink and runs to where the brooms are (usually about ten yards away). He then has to put his forehead on top of the broom stick and run round it ten times: once he has done this he must try and run back to his team and tag the next member of his team who does exactly the same. The winning side is obviously the first back.

Many major problems arise in this game and it is amazing that how ever hard people concentrate they still cannot manage to run in a straight line!!?!

40 · Commander

This is definitely a game for a large group of people and is a game based on 'Simon Says.'

Before the game starts a Chairman or 'Commander' as he is known, is selected, and he should be very proficient at the game. Also a 'Chief Sneak' should be chosen who should be relatively sharp, as it is his job to spot any mistakes made.

The game is best played around a large table and the game starts once the Commander says 'game on,' from then on everyone must be quiet. Then everything the Commander says which is prefixed with the word 'commander,' must be followed by the participants.

For example, you would usually start by sitting down with the palms of your hands out in front of you and the Commander might say 'Commander biblibobs,' which is when you move the fingers of your hands up and down quickly; then the Commander might say 'Commander high,' so you would raise your hands up, and then he might say 'Commander low,' and then you lower your hands, so your fingers are pointing to the floor. All this should be done very quickly and the Commander may continue doing this a few times and suddenly say a command without commander before it, and anyone caught disobeying will be punished usually by a small fine.

As well as 'biblibobs,' and 'high and low,' the Commander should use other commands like 'high biblibobs' which are arms raised and hands biblibobbing; Commander 'very high' when you all stand up and raise your hands high; Commander 'even higher,' when you stand on a chair and once again raise your hands.

Other suggested actions include:- 'Commander surfing' - all stand on chairs and pretend you are surfing.

'Commander canoeing' - same as above but paddling.

'Commander swimming' - same as above but swimming.

A great one to use to liven things up are songs. For example, 'Commander Hawaii - Five- O:-' you sing the theme to the infamous programme and simulate swimming and canoeing actions.

'Commander American Pie:-' you sing the chorus of the great song 'American Pie' by Don Maclean.

There must be silence during the game with only the Commander allowed to speak. If a mistake is made and the Chief Sneak spots it, then he tells the Commander who dishes out the fine. If the Chief Sneak does not spot the mistake but one of the players does, then that person may address the Chief Sneak using a predetermined signal like maybe right hand on head or two fingers up your nose. The Chief Sneak will then tell the Commander, and the fine will be dished out.

The Commander may only be directly addressed if the Chief Sneak makes a mistake and, probably to general public clamour, the Chief Sneak should be treated severely!!?!

Finally if the Commander fails to catch someone out during a single go then he must voluntarily drink.

Good Luck!!?!

41 · Pass the Balloon

You fill a balloon with water and then the participants stand in a circle, preferably alternate sexes.

The idea is to pass the balloon to the person next to you without using your hands or arms in any way, and without dropping it. The best way of doing this is by lodging the balloon under your chin and then trying to pass it. This can be a tricky manoeuvre but provides many laughs. Whoever drops the balloon will get soaking wet, plus have to drink a fine.

42 · The Toilet Game

Can be played with any number of people and is basically a very simple game.

You go for a night out and the first person to go to the toilet becomes 'boy' for the evening. 'Boy' basically means that this person has to act as a waiter for everyone else for the whole evening. Within this role he also has to wear his clothes inside out with obviously his underpants outside his trousers plus his tie around his head just to bring further humiliation upon the poor soul!!?! It is a harsh penalty and so beware keep those legs crossed!!?!

The Toilet Game

43 · The Jug Game

You need a jug filled with a suitable liquid and a large number of people.

To start playing, you pass the jug around the circle with each person drinking as little or as much as he likes directly out of the jug.

Sounds fairly simple? Well the object is to get someone to buy the next jug. This can only occur when one person finishes off the jug and then it is the person who has the penultimate drink who must buy the next one. Therefore as you can see it is a fairly tactical game, because when there is a loser that person must immediately get another jug, and then the game continues straight away. It is fairly intriguing because if there is about one fifth of the jug left, you must decide whether to finish this off or risk whether the next person in line will do so or not!!?! If that person finishes it off then you would have to buy the next jug and thus incur the expense!!?!

Therefore you have to weigh up the option of drinking a lot and feeling a little bit queasy, or having to pay a lot of cash. The choice could be yours!!?!

44 · Pub Golf

You need a town with a number of pubs and a large group. You then designate your route with each pub being one hole. Each pub is a Par 3 which means you have three attempts to down your drink. A lot of people like to go for holes in one at every pub. This is very commendable, but you can come unstuck later on?

Also, every time you go to the toilet you lose a stroke or a lot more if you are playing 'The Toilet Game!!?!' (Explained above).

In at least two of the pubs you must have a chaser to go with your drink, and these pubs are rated Par 4.

It is best to have a score card for yourself, with the winner having the lowest score, and the prizes should be worked out beforehand. Generally prizes should be of the liquid variety and plenty of it!!?!

45 · Bunnies

This is a game for a large group of people.

To play this game you must know how to do a simple 'bunny' which is done by putting your thumbs on your temples and wiggling your fingers about. To do a half 'bunny' you use one hand to do the wiggling.

You start the game by doing general hovers which are arms out and fingers moving up and down. Then the Chairman points at another player, and that player must do a 'bunny' motion, and the players either side must do a half 'bunny motion' according to which side the main 'bunny' is. For example, if you are sitting to the right of the 'bunny,' then you do a half 'bunny' with your left hand which is your thumb on your left temple and fingers wiggling.

The player who is the 'bunny' has to point at someone else to make them 'bunny.' He does this by taking his hands off his temples and pointing with his fingers.

To add spice to the game the person who is 'bunny' is allowed to dummy his pointing once per go, but his hands must not come off his temples when doing this.

If anyone falls for a dummy then they drink and if anyone fails to do a half 'bunny' then they drink. The Chairman must keep a firm grip on the proceedings!!?!

46 · Aliens

A game which definitely requires a sense of humour and a shedding of any inhibitions.

You all sit in a circle facing each other. One player is elected to start, he then must perform an impression of an alien life-form, with facial and physical impressions as well as a suitable 'noise.' After a short period of time (up to the 'impressionist') he must stop all actions and immediately point to another player in the circle who must instantaneously begin his impression. Again after a period he stops and points to another player and so the game continues.

The Chairman must allocate fines for a) any hesitation by players, b) any impressions which are deemed to be too similar to previous impressions and c) any player not giving a '100%' performance.

Note:- This game is guaranteed to annoy any landlord to the extent that most games result in the removal of all players to another pub.

47 · Slaps

A game for any number of players which keeps everyone thinking. To start everyone must sit around a table and place their hands flat on the table with their arms interlinked. The person who starts, states the direction of play and slaps one hand down on the table. The next person then has to slap and so on in that direction without hesitation. This continues until someone either slaps twice, three, four, or five times. For example:-

• A double slap changes the direction of play.

- A triple slap means continuing in the same direction but jumping one hand.
- A quadruple slap means everybody has to stand up and take a drink, left handed drinking of course.
- Finally a fifth slap means that everybody must stand up and sing a line from a pre-determined song like:- The 'Eagles' and their classic song 'Hotel California,' or, 'Status Quo' and their fine tune 'Rockin' all over the world.'

There are various fines for mistakes/hesitation, and you should gradually increase the speed of the game.

48 · Knights, Castles, Princes

This is a game for a large number of people and definitely needs male/female participation. This game requires one Chairman shouting out the commands which are as follows:-

- 'Knights' - The man lifts the woman in cradle fashion.
- 'Castles' - The man gives the woman a piggy back.
- 'Princes' - The woman straddles the man.

These are the basic commands, and once everyone is familiar with these, then everyone must pair off and the game can commence.

Music is played and everyone walks around in a large circle until the music stops, then the Chairman shouts one of the three commands. If a couple do the wrong command then they are out and have to drink a fine. If everyone does the right command then the last pair to complete it drops out and drinks. Often the competitors tend to 'collapse' during the game due to either the weight of the lady partner, or just general laughter!!?! Thus it is fairly easy to distinguish who has come last.

The game is played until there is only one couple left, thus they are the winners and become 'King and Queen' for the night.

49 · Animal Farm

This is a game for a large number of people and requires an imaginative chairman, who is able to make up a story as he goes along.

Each participant takes the name of a farmyard animal, then the chairman begins telling the story and mentioning the names of the different animals. Each time a persons farmyard animal is mentioned, he must make the noise of his animal and then drink one finger, but if he forgets then he must consume double the amount.

Everytime the chairman utters the words 'the farmyard,' everyone must in unison, make their animal noises and then drink a finger!!?!

50 · Bullshit

This game is best played with a large number of you because this will result in mass confusion!!?!

Each person selects an animal and tells everyone the animal chosen. It is important to remember everybody's animal name otherwise it could be costly. The game is started by the chairman shouting out one of the animal names plus 'shit.' For example 'sheepshit.' Then the person whose animal was used replies 'bullshit;' then the chairman says 'whose shit,' then the other person says another animal name and it carries on like that.

For example say there is a cat, cow, dog, goose. If the person who is the cow says 'dogshit' then the person who is a dog replies 'bullshit,' then the cow replies 'whose shit,' then the dog must say another animal, say 'gooseshit.' The person who is a goose then must reply 'bullshit,' then the dog says 'whose shit,' and the goose says another animal name etc etc etc.

One rule is you cannot repeat the animal name you are conversing with.

Best played at high speed because then mistakes are made much more frequently!!?!

Any crass mistakes like replying with the wrong reply, hesitation or using an animal name which does not exist results in a large drinking fine of normally between two and four fingers!!?!

51 · Boat Race

An old favourite of many an evening and a game for as many people as possible, but you must have equal numbers on each side.

Boat Race

You have two teams who line up facing each other preferably pairing off against one another. Each player has a large drink and the game is started at one end with two opposing team members downing their drinks. Once they have finished, they must put their empty glasses on their heads and the next person begins.

Obviously the winning side is the one that downs its drinks the quickest. It is then usually etiquette for the losers to buy the winners a drink or to have a rematch!!?!

52 · Spin the Bottle

A very simple traditional drinking game and can be played with as many people as you want.

All you do is put a bottle in the middle of the table/floor and spin it, whoever it points to has to drink a fine or take a swig out of the bottle you are spinning.

A good hearty spin must be enacted every time otherwise accusations of cheating will be flying around and this would inevitably prove extremely costly to the person concerned!!?!

53 · Rats

Best played with a large group. Each player gets a bottle top/cap, makes a hole in it, puts a long bit of string through the hole and ties it on.

All the bottle tops or 'Rats' are placed tightly in the middle with the participants holding the strings at the edge of the table. One person, who is known as the 'catcher,' does not have a 'Rat' but has a cup/bowl just large enough to fit over all the 'Rats' when they are placed in the middle.

He holds the cup face down at the edge of the table and the object is to catch as many of the 'Rats' as possible while they are still in the middle. The catcher counts down 'three, two, one, go.' Every time he catches one that person has to drink four fingers then drop out, and every time he fails to catch one he has to drink a finger.

Basically the people holding the strings, who will be crouching at the edge of the table, have to pull them away as quickly as possible so that their 'Rats' are not caught, otherwise they must face the consequences. Anyone deemed to be pulling their 'Rat' away too early must drink the four finger fine and still remain in the game!!?!

This game tends to get a little bit violent and aggressive especially as the evening wears on!!?! The catcher must be changed once he has caught all the 'Rats' but only then!!?!

54 · Blind-fold Game

You split into two teams and at one end of the room there is a table with a drink on it for each member of the team. Then one member of each team is blindfolded and turned around ten times, they then have to try and get to the table and down their drink. Once this has been 'safely' negotiated they return to their team and hand the blindfold to the next person, who attempts to do exactly the same.

All sounds fairly simple? Well the trick to this game is teamwork, in that one member of the team must direct the person who is blindfolded, otherwise chaos will reign. The losing team must shout the winners a drink.

Warning:- This game is best played at a party or 'sports' club because breakages and general accidents are always imminent!!?!

55 · Flexible Friends

This is a bit of a personal game and so it is best played with a mixed gender and preferably alternate sexes.

Someone donates a credit card and you have to pass it to the person on your left using your mouth only, with the catch being you have to suction it on your lips in order to pass it. Basically the card has to be flat against your lips, with the trick being that one person sucks while the other blows!!?! If the card is then dropped that means a stiff fine.

Many awkward positions tend to unfurl themselves during this game which make it extremely amusing!!?!

Flexible Friends

56 · Straw Boat Race

This is basically the same as a normal 'Boat Race' except that each participant uses a straw. It is best played with an equal number of people on each side. Plenty of encouragement is required from team members because it tends to be a slow and hazardous procedure, but you will feel exhilarated once you have achieved it!!?! Once again the losers should shout the winners a drink.

Warning:- It is not advisable to play this game too many times in an evening!!?!

57 · Match Box Game

This is a game preferably for a large group of people. You
need a matchbox, a drink each and a decent sized table so
that everyone can sit around it.

The object is to throw the matchbox over your drink so that it
lands on the table. If it lands on its side then it is two fingers to
the next person; if it lands on its end then it is four fingers; and
if it lands flat then it is nothing.

For example, if the box is thrown on its side then it is two
fingers, if the next person throws it on its side then it is four
fingers to the next person in line, and if he throws it flat then
he has to drink the four fingers. Basically the fingers
accumulate until someone fails with a throw.

If the matchbox is thrown into one of the glasses then the
thrower will have to drink all his drink. If the matchbox is
thrown off the table then the thrower will once again have to
drink the lot!!?!

Beware of playing this game with a large jug in the middle
of the table, because if the matchbox ends up in the jug,
then the thrower will have a lot of drinking to do!!?!

58 · Airports

This is an excellent idea for a party or a bar/ pub crawl and
an infinite number of people can play. Everyone lines up in a
'conga style' formation with the 'Captain' at the front. When
everyone is settled you move off to a room in the house or a
pub/bar. Each room or pub represents an airport of a
country around the world and in each country you visit
everyone must consume a drink of the country's national
tipple. Once this has been negotiated you all, in the conga
fashion, fly onto the next destination, and therefore a global
pub crawl is undertaken.

The more countries you visit the more likelihood there is of a
touch of turbulence and so the Captain has to keep a sharp
eye on his crew and passengers for any fall out or travel
sickness!!?!

59 · Naughty Words

A very unusual game and can be played with as many
people as you want.

It is very simple; all you do is for short periods of the evening,
say fifteen minutes of every hour, each person playing must
end their sentence with a certain rude/obscene word, and if
this is not adhered to then you must take a fine. For example
your word might be 'bollocks' and you might be chatting to
someone who is not in the game and you must end your
sentence with the word 'bollocks.'

For example, 'barman can I have five pints and two
packets of crisps, thanks, bollocks.' This can be pretty
embarrassing but if you do not do it then a severe penalty
must be taken. Also, if your girlfriend walks in the bar, then
you know the proceedings and must be prepared for a
good hard slap!!?!

Warning:- The author does not recommend playing this
game with your parents, grandparents or the local vicar!!?!

Naughty Words

V
Dartboard Games

Darts originated in Britain and millions of people throughout the country play the game regularly. I have included in this section a handful of games which will really 'spice' up your darts evening and provide many hours of entertainment.

60 · Darts Cricket
You need two teams with two/three people per team.

The team batting scores runs by scoring over 40. Therefore every point scored over 40 is a run. The team bowling aims at the 'Bullseye.' The outer ring of the 'Bullseye' is one wicket and a 'Bullseye' is two wickets. Should the batting side hit its own wicket it will thus lose a wicket.

If the bowling side fails to get inside the triple boundary, then they will lose that many runs. For example, if you accidentally hit a double 20 then you would lose 40 runs. If you miss the board totally then that gives away 20 runs.

The game can be played under Test Match conditions with two innings each, and each side having 5 wickets per innings, or the 'One Day' format with just one innings each and five wickets per innings. The team who loses has to consume at least four fingers.

61 · Nearest the Edge of the Dartboard

This is best played with a fairly large number of you. All you do is try to get as near to the edge of the board as is possible without going off it. If you go off the board you automatically drink.

You normally play it with the person who is nearest the edge choosing the drink and the person furthest away or off the board having to drink that drink.

Often it is best to play it a little bit safe because there is always some clown who tends to miss the board.

62 · Killer

The more people the merrier for this game. You each throw a dart with your left hand to decide your number. You then have to hit your number five times to become a killer, with a 'double' counting as two and a 'triple' as three hits. Once you are a killer you can hit the other players' numbers and knock them down.

To totally destroy someone you have to hit them down to minus one. If you hit your own number while you are a killer then you lose one. Basically once you are knocked out you drink and the winner is the last person left in.

63 · Man for Man Darts

Each player has three darts and a number is decided upon which you all go for. The person who gets the least amount of the required number will take a fine. The fines are worked out by splitting the difference of the person who scored the most with the person who scored the least. For example if twenties were the required number and the winner managed four of them, while the last placed person managed only one, then he would consume the difference between the two scores, for example three fingers.

Warning:- Do not play this game if you are a beginner because your game will not improve!!?!

64 · Golf Darts

You play 18 holes using the numbers 1-18 on the board. A triple of the number you are going for is a hole in one; a double is a birdie and the section between the triple and the Bull is a par. The section between the triple and the double is a bogey one over par, hitting the Bull is also a one over par and anywhere else on the board is a triple bogey six.

On this game it is best to take your fines after each hole for example one, two, three fingers. If you get under par then you accumulate minus fingers.

Golf Darts

VI
Games which Run Concurrently
Throughout the evening

Whenever you play 'drinking games' it is always satisfying to be able to get your own back on another member of your group. This section will enable you to do just that and all the games included will make your evening an eventful one and hopefully enable you to have the last laugh!!?!

65 · Watchdog

This game keeps everyone awake throughout the whole evening with the people suffering tending to get a little wearisome as proceedings unfold!!?!

The game is started in a haphazard manner with someone placing a coin in another person's drink. This spells the beginning of the game and marks the start of open warfare!!?! The unfortunate individual with the coin now in his drink must consume what is in front of him, making sure that he collects the coin between his teeth as he finishes the last drops of his drink. Then, at any time during the evening he can try and place the coin in someone else's drink. If he succeeds, then they consume, but if he loses the coin in an attempt to get someone else, then he once again must quaff.

66 · Compulsory Cards

These are ideal accompaniments to a rugby, football, cricket touring side or to any large groups of people.

Any kind of cards are handed out to those on the tour/in the group, and you normally give each person three cards for the duration of the tour. Then a card can be played at any time during the trip and whatever is suggested must be done or face a very heavy fine, which must be a predetermined one. Some typical suggestions are:-

- Compulsory 'down in ones!!?!'
- Compulsory 'dead ants,' for example everyone lies on their backs with feet and arms waving in the air like a dead ant!!?!
- Compulsory 'singing.'
- Compulsory 'lying!!?!'

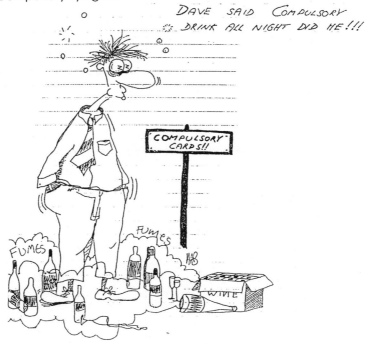

67 · Odd One Out

A simple but effective game and one to play when everyone is not expecting it.

What you do is, if you are sitting with a group of friends one person, who maybe feeling a bit bored, will suddenly stand up and say 'one,' then someone else must individually stand up and say 'two' and then another person 'three' etc etc. But two people must not stand up at the same time or they have to down the rest of their drink and the last person to stand up out of the whole group drinks a three finger fine!!?!

68 · Peg it

This game is best played with a large group of people and should be played at all sorts of social gatherings like stag nights, banquets, wedding receptions etc, etc!!?!

You play using a clothes peg, with the object of the game being for one person to attach the peg to someone else without that person knowing about it. Then someone very loudly shouts 'Peg it,' everyone in the room will quickly check themselves for the peg and there is a ten second time limit to

do so. If the peg is not found on the person's body then he will have to drink what he has got in front of him. If the peg is found then the person who shouted 'Peg it' has to drink.

If the person is caught attaching the peg, by the man he is attempting to put it onto, then he has to drink. Finally if the peg drops off before 'Peg it' is called, then once again the person who attached the peg drinks.

It is best to 'Peg' someone who has just brought a fresh drink because then, if you succeed he will shortly be visiting the bar again!!?!

69 · Burp Game

This game carries on throughout the evening and so everyone must always be on their toes!!?! It is very simple in that every time a member of the group happens to burp, everyone must put one of their hands on their forehead. Anyone who does not remember to do this, automatically gets a good hard slap on the forehead from all members of the group. It is very unsportsmanlike to let out a burp on purpose and anyone thought to be doing so can either be hauled in front of the judge, or made to take an automatic drinking fine!!?! You have been warned!!?!

70 · The Jaffa Cake Game

This game tends to be one of those which keeps recurring throughout the evening, thus keeping everyone on their toes.

The game commences when someone manages to get a Jaffa cake in your drink. You then have fifteen seconds to get it out using only your tongue and teeth, while everyone else will be counting down and the pressure really will be on. No hands are allowed whatsoever.

If you succeed you just eat the Jaffa cake, but if you fail you have to down your drink plus the Jaffa cake. The victim then gets given a fresh Jaffa cake for his revenge on anyone in the group, so beware!!?!

VII
Games for Smaller Groups

Often an evening is spent with just a few of your friends and a quiet, polite evening develops. Well this section will change all that!!?! It is aimed at the smaller groups of people, for example between two and twelve people. The games included will add a different meaning to the term 'a quiet night out.' Raucous behaviour will certainly ensue and laughter will be aplenty!!?!

71 · Drink While You Think
This game is best played with two or more people.

To play you have to decide on a topic, say famous sportsmen and then one person will start drinking his drink until he has thought of a name in this field. He then says that name and the next person continues by using the first letter of the surname to start the christian name of another famous sportsman. Confused!!?! For example if one person said Ian Bothan then the next person would start with the letter 'B' and say a name like Bobby Charlton, and remember all the thinking is done whilst you are consuming your drink.

There is a slight catch to this game because if a name is said where the christian name and surname start with the same letter, then the direction changes. For example,

Graham Gooch, a 'G' starts both the christian name and surname, thus the direction changes.

Some suggested topics:-

- Famous sportsmen.
- Famous sportswomen.
- Famous show business people.
- Famous pop stars.

72 · Spoof

Most definitely a 'gentleman's' game with no football hooligan behaviour allowed. Best played with four to six players although any number can play. Three coins are required by each player and after holding them behind your backs you hold out one fist with either 0, 1, 2 or 3 coins in. The idea is to guess the total number of coins in the fists. For example with six players, the calls will be between 0 and 18. You take it in turns to call and all the calls must be different.

Once everyone has called, the fists are opened and the coins added up. The person who calls correctly is out unless they display football hooligan behaviour such as cheering or raising a fist in which case they are back in the game!!?! The game is repeated until only two players are left for a head to head to decide the ultimate loser, who should have a hefty drinking fine of normally four fingers or more.

This game is strictly a 'gentleman's' game and therefore no cheating or false calling is allowed. An example of this behaviour would be if you had '2' coins in your fist and you call 'one.' This is deemed ungentlemanly behaviour because it is a false call and should receive the necessary punishment.

73 · Tickled Pinkies

This game sorts out the men from the boys and the women from the girls.

Only people with very ticklish feet are allowed to participate in this game!!?! The object of the game is to see how long you can 'hold out' while your feet are being intensely tickled by up to three 'ticklers.'

It is best to sit on a comfy chair with one foot on a 'tickling' stool. You need a stop watch to time your endurance with the winner having the best time, while the losers suffer the further punishment of a stiff drinking fine.

Caution:- Many tears will be shed!!?!

Tickled Pinkies

74 · Fuzzy Duck

This is a favoured game of many a drinking community, basically because chaos is bound to set in?

You all sit round a table and one person states the direction he wants to go and says 'fuzzy duck,' the next player repeats this and so on until one player decides to say 'does he.' (Note anyone can say this). From then on the words 'ducky fuzz' must be repeated again until someone says 'does he,' where the words are swapped back to the original 'fuzzy duck.'

This might all sound pretty straight forward, but both 'fuzzy duck' and 'ducky fuzz' are both very similar sounding, and once the slurring stage of the evening is upon you, all types of problems will occur!!?!

Large drinks should be consumed for general mistakes, swearing and nervous breakdowns!!?!

75 · Rising Sun

This is a verbal version of 'Slaps' but played with a Japanese emphasis.

The rules are, if you say 'Yip' then that goes the way that you stated; 'Yong' changes the direction; 'Yang' goes the same way but misses one person; 'Ying', you all stand up and drink a finger; finally 'Yeng' means that you all stand up and sing the chorus from that classic 'Vapours' song of 1980,'Turning Japanese.'

All these calls are to be done at high speed with drinking penalties for hesitation, mis-pronunciation and calling when it is not your call.

76 · Obstacles

This game is not for the faint hearted and basically requires four or more people.

To play you need three glasses, two dice and a counter. The glasses are spaced out in a line with each glass being filled with different liquids.

The first player rolls the dice and he has to say if he thinks he will roll higher or lower with his next throw. Whatever he says will determine the sequence of high or low to come. For example, if he throws a '6' to start off with, he will obviously call lower. A '5' might then be thrown and he will move past the first glass, but then he will have to throw higher, due to the sequence high/low. He can only move on until a '6' is thrown and each time he fails to achieve this he has to drink, with the glass obstacle being filled up each time he makes a mistake.

Once the 'three' drinks have been successfully negotiated you have the choice of either attempting to re-negotiate the 'obstacles,' or to drink all 'three' drinks, a tricky decision?

77 · Ten Guesses

You pick a sport or subject like rugby, football, politics and then one person in the group has to think of a 'famous' person within that certain sport or area. The people playing then have ten 'free' questions to try and work out who the person is. The guy must answer 'yes' or 'no' to the questions. If the person's name is not found after ten questions, then every question asked after that is one finger of a drink.

If the 'famous person' is guessed before ten questions are asked, then the guy thinking of the person must drink the amount of guesses deducted from ten. For example if four guesses are taken then he must drink six fingers.

78 · My Old Grandma

This is a game of memory and repetition. You start the game by saying 'my old grandma went down the market and brought a basket of ...' for example 'apples,' then the next person must say 'my old grandma went down the market and brought a basket of apples' and for example 'pears.' Therefore each person has to add on an extra item, but you also must remember to repeat what has been said before. If any items are not repeated you must drink at least two fingers for every item missed out.

79 · Touch Too Much

Can be played with two or more people, preferably a slightly larger group.

You need a sheet of tissue paper, an elastic band and a glass. Place the tissue paper over the glass and attach it using the elastic band. Then place a coin in the middle of the tissue.

You then take a cigarette and take it in turns to burn a hole in the tissue paper, trying not to let the coin drop into the glass. The person who burns the hole which drops the coin is the loser and then downs a drink.

This game can turn into a very tactical affair because the risk takers amongst you will burn holes close to the coin and thus dramatically increase the problems for the next person!!?!

Touch Too Much

80 · Sing a Subject

This is a game guaranteed to liven up proceedings as long as everyone puts all their effort into it.

What you do is a Chairman picks a certain subject, topic, colour etc, everyone then has to think of a song with that subject, topic etc contained within it and then sing a line from that song. For example, you might choose the colour 'blue' and what springs to mind could be Elvis Presley's 'Get off my Blue Suede Shoes.'
   Another example might be the Chairman choosing 'garments of clothing,' and thus someone might choose 'Right Said Fred's', 'I'm too sexy.'
   Everyone in the group must think of a song or face dire consequences. Fines should be dished out for unconvincing singing.
   Once everyone has become proficient at singing one line from a song, you then must try and sing a whole verse, and major problems will definitely result!!?!

81 · Harry

All you do is get in a circle and the first person starts it off by looking at a member of the group and saying to that person 'Harry,' then that person will reply 'yes Harry' and the first person says 'tell Harry.' Then that person continues with exactly the same lines on another person in the group. If you are talking to girls then they are Harriettes?

If someone mucks it up then they immediately become 'Harry one spot' or 'Harriette one spot.' The second person to muck it up becomes 'Harry two spot' or 'Harriette two spot' etc etc.
   After it has been around the group a few times the game should be speeded up, plus you should all swap seats and then real confusion sets in!!?!

82 · Syllables

This is a game along the lines of 'Drink while you think.' Basically you nominate how many syllables you want to be in a surname, nominate a topic, and then all you have to do is take it in turns, whilst drinking, to come up with surnames with the required syllables. The last letter of the surname is the letter for the next person to start with.

For example:- You might choose two syllables and have say famous sports people. Then the first person might say 'David Gower' in which case 'R' would be the next starting letter of the surname, and the next person might say 'Viv Richards,' for example the surname begins with an 'R' and it is a two syllable surname. Finally if the surname ends in a vowel then it changes the direction of the game.

83 · Roman Centurion

Basically a great game for three or more of you.

What you need to know in this game is that to go to the left you hit the left part of your chest with your right fist and to go to the right you hit the right part of your chest with your left fist.

Someone starts by going right or left and then the next person can carry on the same direction or reverse the direction. When it gets to the fifth person he then holds his hands above one another so that the fingers are pointing sideways and which ever way the top hands fingers are pointing is the way it goes. For example, if your right hand is on top of your left then the direction will be to the left. When it reaches seven, the seventh man points at another player and then it starts from one again.

It is basically a game going from numbers one to seven and just continues going round. It sounds very simple but most of the simple games tend to create havoc!!?! Drinking fines for hesitation and stupidity.

84 · Sinking Glass

What you need for this game is a glass and a jug of water.

You float the glass in the jug of water and then take it in turns to put as much/little water in the floating glass as you like, with the person who makes it hit the bottom losing.

Large fines should be dished out for the losers and you must remember that you should not be too rash when putting the water in the glass because some glasses sink rather quickly!!?!

85 · The Slapping Clapping Clicking Game

You start this game by doing general hovers with both hands (for example biblibobs, explained earlier), then the Chairman shouts 'drop them!' Everyone first slaps their thighs, then claps, then clicks the fingers of their right and then their left hand and this is the routine for the whole game so it is best to remember it quickly! The chairman will then say 'give me,' but this can only be said on the clicking of the fingers; then 'names of' (only on the finger clicking); 'famous people' (only on the finger clicking), 'to my left, Robin Williams,' and then the next person must continue etc etc.

You must remember that you can only speak on the clicking of the fingers and at no other time.

Also any subjects can be used and the harder the better. Some suggested topics:-

- Types of Drink.
- Famous female models.
- Christmas No 1's.
- Makes of Condoms.

As you get better at this game it is best to speed things up, then more mistakes are made, and thus more drinking!!?!

86 · Cardinal Puff

This game is best played with a small group of you and each participant must be very observant and alert at all times.

Everyone sits around a table and the Chairman starts the game by standing up with his full glass and announcing:- 'I drink to the health of Cardinal Puff.'

He then sits down, places his glass on the table, taps the table with one finger of his left hand and then one finger of his right hand. He then taps the underside of the table once with each hand. Then he taps his right leg with his right hand and his left leg with his left hand. He then picks up his glass holding it with one finger and his thumb, takes one sip and taps the glass down once on the table.

He then says:-

'I drink to the health of Cardinal Puff for the second time.' then he repeats the above sequence, tapping the table twice with two fingers, tapping the underside of the table twice, tapping both his legs twice and then holding his glass with two fingers and thumb and finally placing the glass down twice.

Then he announces:-

'I drink to the health of Cardinal Puff for the third and final time.'

Everything is done as above but three times, and once this has all been done, he sits down and the next person must try his luck at drinking the Cardinals health.

Any mistakes result in that person starting again and so it can be a long and difficult process for many people. It is not a game for the faint hearted!!?!

Cardinal Puff

87 · Giraffes

All you need to play is a matchbox.

You start by someone kneeling down with their hands behind their backs. Whilst in this position he must try, by bending forwards towards the ground, to pick up the outside of an empty matchbox, which has been placed on the floor in front of them, using only his nose and without toppling over. If everyone achieves this then the matchbox is moved a little further away.

If a person topples over then he must drink a fine of three fingers and then drop out. The winner is the person who manages the furthest distance without toppling over.

88 · Conceal the Coin
This game is best played with six people.

You need two teams of three who sit opposite each other. You decide who is to go first by a simple 'hic hac hoc' between captains, and then you play. One team has the coin and all their hands go under the table and then the coin is transferred to one of the six hands. When they are all ready they simultaneously bring their hands flat down on the table and the opposing side will have to guess which hand contains the coin. Often when the hands are slapped down on the table, the noise of the coin hitting the table can give a major clue.

Choosing where the coin is, should be done through a process of elimination, and if they are right in this process, for example the coin is in the last hand turned over, then the side hiding the coin has to drink four fingers. If the guessing side fails in its quest for the coin then they must quaff four fingers.

89 · Ibble Dibble
This is a game for a maximum of twelve people with each of the players having a number, starting with one and going up. Then the person who is 'ibble dibble' number one for example says:-

'This is "ibble dibble" number one with no "ibbles or dibbles" calling "ibble dibble" number six with no "ibbles or dibbles," ibble dibble.'

Any mistakes as regards the above wording, the number of 'ibble dibbles' a player has, or undue hesitation will result in a player acquiring an 'ibble dibble' which is a mark placed on the face with the burnt end of a cork. The player must also consume three fingers.

Therefore each mistake made results in an 'ibble dibble.' You must remember how many 'ibble dibbles' you have and how many everyone else has, otherwise chaos reigns! This game usually ends up with numerous participants covered in 'cork marks' due to absolute mayhem!!?!

90 · Peanuts

This is best played with two or more people. The game requires each participant to have a large fizzy drink and a salted peanut. Each participant drops his nut into his drink, it should then drop to the bottom, and the first persons peanut to float to the top is the winner. The losers will then have to consume their drinks.

Experience will count in this game, because you will soon realise that the type of nut used is extremely important, for example dry roasted or ready salted. Also what liquid you are using to race your nut in is crucial! You have been warned!!?!

91 · Dambusters

A good, simple but hilarious 'family' drinking game.

All you do is put a large 'filled' up glass about ten feet away, and take it in turns to try and drop five coins in the glass all in one go?

It sounds easy, but all the coins must somehow be held between your thighs, so you are still able to walk and then aim at your target. Each person always has a different technique and the consequences tend to be hilarious! All the coins must go in and so it can take a number of attempts to achieve this.

The last person to drop his coins in, has to drink what is in the glass!!?!

92 · Armchair Tunnels

This game was discovered in an Officers Mess in Germany where this peculiar sport appeals to a definite aggressive tendency!!?!

Place at least six chairs against each other so that they form a tunnel shape.

Two players compete against each other and the remainder of people present sit on the backs of the chairs, thus stopping any of the chairs moving. The two players start at opposite ends of the room and it is the first player through the tunnel to touch the other end of the room. The result is of course a certain amount of 'foul play' in the tunnel to prevent your opponent from getting through before you.

There are no rules and the loser has to shout the victorious opponent a drink.

93 · Follow my Leader

Each person has to follow what the 'Leader' says. Basically it is a little song with a new line added every time it goes around the group. The song goes like this:-

One red hen.
Two cute ducks.
Three brown bears.
Four running hares.
Five fat females sitting sipping scotch smoking cigarettes.
Six sleazy sluts slinking and sliding in slippery snow.
Seven elongated alligators eating anteaters.
Eight enormous elephants escalating elevators.
Nine naughty nuns nuzzling naughty Nicki's nighties.

So therefore the 'Leader' will start by saying the first line and each individual in turn has to repeat this. Then the 'Leader' says the first and second lines and everyone in turn must repeat what has been said. It continues on like this, so each time a new verse is added, all the previous verses must be spoken as well.

As you can see, as the song goes on it gets a little bit more complicated as each verse unfolds. The mistakes are fairly rife and much 'quaffing' will be done. This game has a simple equation:- the more you drink the more mistakes you make and mistakes mean more drinks!!?!

94 · Blowing in the Wind

A game for a number of people. All you need is a pack of cards and an empty glass. You place the pack of cards on top of the glass and you take it in turns to blow cards off the pack using only one 'breath' per go.

You must blow a minimum one card off per go, otherwise you drink. If you blow all the cards off the glass then you also lose and take a four finger fine.

   If only one card is left on the glass then the person whose turn it is will automatically lose and suffer the indignity of having to consume six fingers!!?!

95 · Frogs

Best played with four or more people and fairly late on in the evening.

All you do is the chairman says 'one frog, two eyes, four legs, plop into the pond.' The second person says 'two frogs; four eyes; eight legs, plop, plop into the pond.' It carries on accumulating until someone makes a mistake, or someone is too slow with their go. This might all sound rather simple but I can assure you that major problems always occur and a blankness often envelops your mind as the game rolls on!!?!

   Every mistake should mean at least a two finger fine if not more?

96 · Zoom

To play 'Zoom' you are required to learn three words, firstly 'Zoom,' secondly 'Swartz,' finally 'Befidiliano' and of course their meanings. The idea is that you pass an imaginary ball around the circle by making eye contact with another player, and making one of the calls. 'Zoom' is the most basic where you pass the ball (control) to the person you are looking at. 'Swartz' is if you want to pass the ball straight back to the person who passed it to you. (You must also look at them). On the other hand if you want to pass back to them but try to catch them out 'Befidiliano' is your call where you look at someone else, but really it is a dummy pass back to the person who passed it to you. This can also catch out the person you looked at, as they should ignore your call.

   A quick recap is required at this stage.

'Zoom' if you just want to pass the ball on.

'Swartz' if you want to pass it back to the person who just gave you it and thus change the direction of play.

'Befidiliano,' a dummy pass where you look at someone else but it is going back to the person who just passed it to you.

Confusion always sets in and two finger fines should be readily consumed for any mistakes.

97 · Quarters

Best played with three or more people.

All the players sit around a table with glasses of drink. The drinks are all tightly bunched in the middle of the table, with an extra glass right in the middle.

The object is to bounce the coin on the table into another persons glass. If you are successful then that person drinks. If you get the coin in your own glass then you drink.

If you succeed in getting it in the middle glass then everyone must down their drink and the last person to finish, drinks the middle one as well. If the coin is bounced off the table then the guilty party has to consume. This game can take a little practice and so do not be dismayed if you initially find yourself drinking your fair share, because practice makes perfect!!?!

Quarters

98 · Criss-Cross

All you do here is if there are a group of you sitting/standing around, each person must be addressed by the name of the person on your right for a set period of time, or alternatively you can each take the name of a 'famous' person and have to be addressed by that name for the set period of time. Any mistakes on names means a fine!!?!

Some suggested 'famous' group names:-

• Characters from the 'A' Team.

• Characters from Coronation Street.

• Characters from Dallas.

• Characters from Grange Hill.

99 · Hi Ho

To play this game you must know the tune and words of 'Hi Ho.' This goes 'hi ho, hi ho, it's off to work we go, with a shovel and a pick and a walking stick hi ho, hi ho hi ho, hi ho, hi ho it's off to work' etc etc.

Once this is known you each get two glasses/bottles and hold them on the table in either hand. Then you start singing the song and each time you have sung two words you pass the bottles to the person on your right and he will do the same to the person on his right etc etc. You do this until you get to the part of the song where it says; 'with a shovel and a pick and a walking stick.' On this part of the song you pick up the two bottles which have been passed to you and instead of passing them on, you move them to your right but bring them back and do this five times (for example every two words). After the word 'stick' you once again release the bottles to the person on your right. The song continues going round and mistakes will be made which will obviously result in large drinking fines for all concerned!!?!

100 · Bottled-Up

This is an entertaining game to be played at any time during the evening and all you need are two bottles.

What you do is place your heels against a wall, then crawl out using the bottles as your only support to keep you off the ground, and your heels must remain touching the wall throughout. You stretch as far out as you can, place one bottle down, then try to get back to the wall and stand up. This all must be done without falling over!!?!

The person who gets the bottle out the furthest is the winner and the losers consume four fingers.

101 · 3 Man

This is a game with a number of rules but they are easy to pick up.

You need two normal dice and for certain rolls and numbers you are required to do certain commands.

If '11' is rolled then the person next to throw drinks.

If '7' is rolled then the person the other side of the dice thrower drinks.

If a '6 and 3' are thrown then everyone has to put a fist to their cheek, the last to do so drinks a finger; if '6 and 2' are thrown then two fingers are put to your cheek and the last person to do so drinks. If a '6 and 1' are thrown then one finger goes to your cheek and the last man drinks. If the wrong amount of fingers are put against a cheek then the guilty parties automatically drink.

You become the '3 man' if you roll the number '3' or your dice add up to '3,' (for example 1+2). Once you are the '3' man then every time a '3' is rolled you drink, except if a double '3' is thrown or a '4 and 3.' You can only get out of the '3 man' if you throw a '3.' The '3 man' would then continue to the next person who manages to throw a '3.'

If a double is thrown then the thrower may nominate the digits of one of these dice as fingers to one or more participants. If say double '6' is thrown then he can give all six fingers to one person, or give three fingers to two people etc.

Finally you have a '9' man; this is when someone rolls '9' they have to drink a finger and then the next person in line drinks when the next '9' is thrown.

You have to concentrate very hard when playing this game and your luck must be in!!?!

Index

Notes

Notes

Notes

Notes